OAuth 2.0
Learn OAuth in a simple way

Table of Contents

Introduction 5

Chapter 1- Creating an OAuth2 authenticated API 6

Chapter 2- Client Credentials 15

Chapter 3- Authorization Code Grant Types 23

Chapter 4- Saving Token 33

Chapter 5- User Login with OAuth 49

Chapter 6- OAuth with Facebook 57

Conclusion 69

Introduction

The OAuth 2.0 standard is very useful when it comes to the access of resources of the server by the client apps. It makes this process very easy to accomplish. You should learn how to use this standard. In today's world, most people are on Facebook, Twitter, and other forms of social media. This standard can assist such users to access third-party websites. In this book, we will explore most of the aspects which are associated with this standard. The book has been made simple for everyone to understand, even the beginners. Enjoy reading it!

Chapter 1- Creating an OAuth2 authenticated API

In this chapter, we will create a simple app and then test it by use of OAuth-plugin, devise, and rspec.

Rails app

First, launch your terminal. You can then create a folder and give it a name. This is where you will keep both the provider and the consumer. The following sequence of commands can be used:

mkdir OAuth && cd OAuth
rails new provider
cd provider

The OAuth-plugin gem can then be added to the Gemfile. A devise to provide authentication should be used. If you need to do your testing using RSpec, it should be added at this time. This is shown below:

gem 'devise'
gem "OAuth-plugin", ">= 0.4.0.rc2"
group :test do
**   gem 'rspec-rails'**
end

The OAuth-plugin can then be installed by executing the command "bundle install."

For the users of respect, execute the command given below:

rails g rspec:install

For devise users, create the devise install and the user as follows:

rails generate devise:install
rails generate devise User

The next step should involve creation of the aouth provider. This can be done as shown below:

rails g OAuth_provider --test-framework=rspec

You can then migrate the database as follows:

rake db:migrate

The test database can be done as follows:

rake db:test:prepare

After the above step, some files will be generated, but will need some changes. The first step should involve deletion of the file "spec/controllers/OAuth_clients_controller_spec.rb." Since we are discussing OAuth2, the file "/spec/models/OAuth_token_spec.rb" should also be deleted or removed. The following should also be added to the file "config/routes.rb":

```
root :to => "OAuth_clients#index"
```

The following methods should also be added to the file "app/controllers/application_controller.rb" for things to work correctly:

```
def current_user=(user)
 current_user = user
end
```

The following should then be added to the user model:

```
has_many :client_applications
has_many                                    :tokens,
:class_name=>"OAuth2Token",:order=>"authorized
_at desc",:include=>[:client_application]
```

The following attr-accessor should be added to the file "app/models/OAuth_token.rb":

```
attr_accessor :expires_at
```

Then create the following alias:

```
alias :login_required :authenticate_user!
```

The following should then be added to the file "config/application.rb":

require 'OAuth/rack/OAuth_filter'
config.middleware.use OAuth::Rack::OAuthFilter

For the purpose of real testing, make use of factories. The four fixture files can be grabbed from spec/fixtures.

After inclusion of the above files, the rspec can be executed to test whatever we have so far. This can be done as shown below:

bundle exec rspec spec

A basic rspec test should then be created, and this is to be used for testing so as to know more about your API call. Our API calls in this case will need us to have a valid OAuth token. We should then create a base controller and a data controller. These can be created as shown below:

rails g controller API::V1::Base
rails g controller API::V1::Data

The DataController should then be changed to expand the API::V1::BaseController. This can be done as shown below:

class Api::V1::DataController <
Api::V1::BaseController
end

The routes can then be created by adding the following to the file "config/routes.rb":

```
namespace :api do
  namespace :v1 do
    match "data" => "data#show"
  end
end
```

A show action will then be needed in the data controller. This is shown below:

```
def show
  respond_with ({:super_secret => "OAuth_data"})
end
```

One should also specify the formats which the controllers responds to in the base controller. This is shown below:

```
respond_to :json, :xml
```

The methods which are to require OAuth should also be specified. The following also needs to be added to the base controllers:

```
OAuthenticate :interactive=>false
```

The client

The following in the "views/OAuth/OAuth2_authorize.html.erb" should be changed:

<p>Do you want to authorize <%= link_to @token.client_application.name,@token.client_application.url %> (<%= link_to @token.client_application.url,@token.client_application.url %>) to access your account?</p>

To the following:

<p>Do you want to authorize <%= link_to @client_application.name,@client_application.url %> (<%= link_to @client_application.url,@client_application.url %>) to access your account?</p>

At this point, you can launch your rails server and then navigate to the directory http://localhost:3000/users/sign_up. Once you have signed up, go to the URL http://localhost:3000/OAuth_clients and then create a client. The client callback_url should be the same to the one which was passed into your app.

The @tokens block in views/OAuth_clients/index.html.erb should be changed to the following:

```erb
<% @tokens.each do |token|%>
  <tr>
    <td><%= link_to token.client_application.name,
token.client_application.url %></td>

    <td><%= token.authorized_at %></td>
    <td> </td>
  </tr>
<% end %>
```

The block @client_applications should be changed to the following:

```erb
<% @client_applications.each do |client|%>
  <div>
    <%= link_to client.name,
OAuth_client_path(client) %>-
    <%= link_to 'Edit',
edit_OAuth_client_path(client) %>
    <%= link_to 'Delete', OAuth_client_path(client),
:confirm => "Do you mean it?", :method => :delete
%>

  </div>
<% end %>
```

The consumer should then be created outside our rails root as shown below:

```
cd ..
mkdir consumer && cd consumer
```

Sinatra and OAuth2 gem should then be installed. The following commands can be used for installation of these:

```
gem install sinatra
gem install OAuth2
```

The following code should then be created, and the API keys replaced with those of the client:

```
require 'sinatra'
require 'json'
require 'OAuth2'
enable :sessions
def client
  OAuth2::Client.new(consumer_key,
consumer_secret, :site => "http://localhost:3000")

end
get "/auth/test" do
  redirect
client.auth_code.authorize_url(:redirect_uri         =>
redirect_uri)

end
get '/auth/test/callback' do
  access_token                                        =
client.auth_code.get_token(params[:code],
:redirect_uri => redirect_uri)

  session[:access_token] = access_token.token
  @message = "Authentication with the server was
successful"
  erb :success
end

get '/yet_another' do
  @message = get_response('data.json')
  erb :success
```

```
end
get '/another_page' do
  @message = get_response('data.json')
  erb :another
end

def get_response(url)
  access_token  =  OAuth2::AccessToken.new(client,
session[:access_token])

JSON.parse(access_token.get("/api/v1/#{url}").body
)
end


def redirect_uri
  uri = URI.parse(request.url)
  uri.path = '/auth/test/callback'
  uri.query = nil
  uri.to_s
end
```

At this point, the required views can be grabbed from CONSUMER/VIEWS.

Chapter 2- Client Credentials

Starting the Command-line Script

The API COOP's is very simple as it has very few endpoints, and we will need one of these in our command-line-script. This is the eggs-collect.

Now that I have a "/cron" directory having a script named "collect_eggs.php," we can get started:

```
// the file collect_eggs.php contents
include __DIR__.'/vendor/autoload.php';
use Guzzle\Http\Client;
// creating the http client (Guzzle)
$http = new Client('http://coop. mysite.com', array(
  'request.options' => array(
    'exceptions' => false,
  )
));
```

Note that the above will do nothing except that we create a client object which will point to the COOP website. We will have to use Guzzle which is a very nice PHP library and this will make it possible for us to make HTTP calls to the COOP API.

The composer should be used for helping us to download the Guzzle. This should be downloaded into the "cron/" directory and then the vendor libraries installed. This is shown below:

php composer.phar install

Our first API request should be made to *"/api/3/eggs-collect."* The 2 represents our COOP user ID. Your number should be different from this. This is shown below:

```php
// collect_eggs.php
// ...
$request = $http->post('/api/2/eggs-collect');
$response = $request->send();
echo $response->getBody();
echo "\n\n";
```

To try it, you have to execute the script on the command line as shown below:

```
php collect_eggs.php
```

This will bow up as shown below:

```json
{
  "error": "access_denied",
  "error_description": "an access token is required"
}
```

Client Credentials Grant Type

Client credentials are the simplest type of OAuth grant type. Only two parties are involved, which are the server and the client. In our case, it will form the COOP API and the command-line script.

In this grant type, we will have no user and the access token that we get will allow us to access our resources under control of our application. When we use this access token for the purpose of making an API request, we will have logged in as the application itself, but not as an individual user. After opening the application which you had created, you will observe a link labeled *"Generate a Token"* and after clicking it, one will be fetched. The credentials of the client will be used for this purpose. This is shown below:

http://coop. mysite.com/token
  ?client_id=Your+Client+Name
  &client_secret=wxyzabc
  &grant_type=client_credentials

At this point, the token can be used for the purpose of taking some actions on behalf of the application, and all will be okay.

Access Tokens in API

The process on how this is done is determined by the API to which we are making the requests. Sending it via the Authorization Bearer header is the most common method which one makes use of. This is shown below:

```
GET /api/barn-unlock HTTP/1.1
Host: coop.mysite.com
Authorization: Bearer ACCESSTOKENHERE
```

The script can then be updated so as to send the header as shown below:

```
// collect-eggs.php
// ...
$accessToken = 'xyz1234abc67740';

$request = $http->post('/api/2/eggs-collect');
$request->addHeader('Authorization',           'Bearer
'.$accessToken);
$response = $request->send();
echo $response->getBody();
echo "\n\n";
```

After running the script again, you will notice that it will run:

```
{
  "action": "eggs-collect",
  "success": true,
  "message": "Hey there! Now look it is executing as
expected, congratulations",
```

```
  "data": 3
}
```

We can also opt to change our ID so that we use the one for a different user. This should make it fail. Consider the example given below:

```
{
  "error": "access_denied",
  "error_description": "You have no access to take this action"
}
```

Technically, when we have tokens from our client credentials, we will be making requests on behalf of the application other than the user. This will mean that the client calls will be made perfect for the purpose of making API calls.

Using Client Credentials to get the Token

Access Tokens will not live forever. The tokens for COOP usually take 24 hours, which is an indication that the script breaks up in the following day.

We can let the client-credentials work be done for us by the website, but it is recommended that we do it for ourselves inside the script. For every OAuth server, there is an API endpoint which can be used for the purpose of requesting access tokens. The Post and URL parameters which are needed can be obtained from the authentication docs of COOP API.

We now need to perform an update of our script so that it makes an API request. Just begin by filling in the POST parameters "*client_id*," "*client_secret*," and "*grant_type*."This is shown below:

```php
// collect-eggs.php
// ...
// this code should be run first before you can request
the eggs-collect //endpoint
$request = $http->post('/token', null, array(

   'client_id'   => 'Brent\'s Lazy CRON Job',
   'client_secret'                                => 'b3t4f02abc711095f77f2gc04ecbd0d3',
   'grant_type'   => 'client_credentials',
));
// making a request to our token url
$response = $request->send();
$responseBody = $response->getBody(true);
var_dump($responseBody);die;
```

// ...

After running the above code and you are lucky, you will see a JSON response having an access token and some other details. These are shown in code given below:

```
{
 "access_token":                          "
b3t4f02abc711095f77f2gc04ecbd0d3",
 "expires_in": 76300,
 "token_type": "Bearer",
 "scope": "chickens-feed"
}
```

This is the access token that we should use other than the one we pasted earlier on. This is shown below:

```
// collect-eggs.php
// ...
// step1: requesting for an access token
$request = $http->post('/token', null, array(
   'client_id'    => 'John\'s Lazy CRON Job',
   'client_secret'                    =>              '
b3t4f02abc711095f77f2gc04ecbd0d3',
   'grant_type'  => 'client_credentials',
));

// making a request to our token url
$response = $request->send();
$responseBody = $response->getBody(true);
$responseArr = json_decode($responseBody, true);
$accessToken = $responseArr['access_token'];

// step2: using the access token for making an API request
```

```php
$request = $http->post('/api/3/eggs-collect');
$request->addHeader('Authorization',        'Bearer
'.$accessToken);
$response = $request->send();
echo $response->getBody();

echo "\n\n";
```

With the above, the running will be smooth. Note that we are refreshing to get a new access token. This means that we will not experience any expiration of the tokens.

Chapter 3- Authorization Code Grant Types

You have already developed your app and stored it in the "-client/" directory. Let us use the PHP server which is already built-in to so as to run the site. This is shown below:

cd client/web
php -S localhost:9000

With the above command, the built-in PHP web server will be started. We will also use the composer in this project.

Redirect to Authorize

You can see the Authorize link on the homepage of the app, and this just displays the message. The code behind the URL is in the file "*src/OAuth2Demo/Client/Controllers/CoopOAuthController. php.*" You do not have to master how it works, but just know that whatever is done will be shown there. This is shown below:

```
// src/OAuth2Demo/Client/Controllers/CoopOAuthController.php
// ...
public function redirectTOAuthorization(Request $request)
{
    die('Hallo there!');
}
```

In authorization grant type, our first step should involve redirecting the user to the specific URL on COOP.

We can then begin to build our URL in the code as shown below:

```
// src/OAuth2Demo/Client/Controllers/CoopOAuthController.php
// ...
public function redirectTOAuthorization(Request $request)
{
```

```php
    $url = 'http://coop.apps.knpuniversity.com/authorize?'.http_build_query(array(

        'response_type' => 'code',
        'client_id' => '?',
        'redirect_uri' => '?',
        'scope' => 'eggs-count profile'
    ));

    var_dump($url);die;
}
```

Our response type in this case is *"code,"* since we are making use of authorization code flow. "token" is also a valid token, and it belongs to a grant type named *"implicit flow."*

We now need to set the URL to "/coop/OAuth/handle." This should be another message which will print a message. This is shown below:

```php
// src/OAuth2Demo/Client/Controllers/CoopOAuthController.php
// ...
public function receiveAuthorizationCode(Application $app, Request $request)

{
    // equivalent to $_GET['code']
    $code = $request->get('code');
    die('Implement this in CoopOAuthController::receiveAuthorizationCode');
}
```

Let us make use of the URL generator other than hard coding the URL. This is shown below:


```
public function redirectTOAuthorization(Request $request)
{
   $redirectUrl = $this->generateUrl('coop_authorize_redirect', array(), true);

   $url = 'http://coop.apps.knpuniversity.com/authorize?'.http_build_query(array(

      'response_type' => 'code',
      'client_id' => 'TopCluck',
      'redirect_uri' => $redirectUrl,
      'scope' => 'eggs-count profile'
   ));
   // ...
}
```


However, once you have made your URL, you should make sure that it is absolute. Now that we have our Authorize URL to the COOP, the user can then be redirected to it as shown below:


```
public function redirectTOAuthorization(Request $request)
{
   // ...
   return $this->redirect($url);
}
```

In my app, the *"redirect"* function is very special, meaning that your code may bring a difference.

The authorization code can also be exchanged for an access token. The query parameter has the name authorization code, and it is unique for the grant type. Note that we are not in need of the access token, but we need the key to enable us to get that. The authorization code will provide us with proof that our application could have an access token.

We now need to copy the code from "collect_eggs.php" and then paste it here. The parameters *"client_id"* and *"client_secret"* should then be changed so that they those are of the new client. This is shown in the code given below:

```
//
src/OAuth2Demo/Client/Controllers/CoopOAuthCon
troller.php
// ...

public                                    function
receiveAuthorizationCode(Application $app, Request
$request)

{
    // equivalent to $_GET['code']
    $code = $request->get('code');
    $http = new Client('http://coop.mysite.com', array(
        'request.options' => array(
            'exceptions' => false,
        )
    ));
    $request = $http->post('/token', null, array(
        'client_id'   => 'TopCluck',
```

```
    'client_secret'                    =>                    '
b3t4fo2abc711095f77f2gco4ecbdod3',
    'grant_type'   => 'authorization_code',
  ));
  // making a request to our token url
  $response = $request->send();
  $responseBody = $response->getBody(true);
  var_dump($responseBody);die;
}
```

The property "/token" will have 2 parameters which are to be used together with the authorization grant type. This can be seen in the COOP API Authentication docs. These parameters are the "code" and "redirect_uri." The parameters *grant_type* to *authorization_code* should also be changed as the description has been done in the docs. Finally, the "$responseBody" can be dumped so as to check on whether the request is working correctly. This is shown below:

```
public                                 function
receiveAuthorizationCode(Application $app, Request
$request)

{
  // similar to $_GET['code']
  $code = $request->get('code');
  // ...
  $request = $http->post('/token', null, array(
    'client_id'    => 'TopCluck',
    'client_secret'                        =>                    '
b3t4fo2abc711095f77f2gco4ecbdod3',
    'grant_type'   => 'authorization_code',
    'code'         => $code,
    'redirect_uri'                         =>                 $this-
>generateUrl('coop_authorize_redirect',        array(),
true),
  ));
```

```
  // ...
}
```

The "*code*" parameter is then key to the authorization flow. Once the request is received by the COOP, the authorization code is checked on whether it is valid or not. The user to which the authorization code belongs should also be known, so that the returned API request will allow us to make requests on behalf of the user. The parameter "*redirect_uri*" is very important for our access code to work effectively. However, COOP does not use it in any way. It is a very good security measure which must be the same as the original "*redirect_uri*" which we used during the process of redirection of the user.

After refreshing, you will notice that the API will give us an error. This is shown below:

```
{
   "error": "invalid_grant",
   "error_description": "The authorization code has expired"
}
```

The authorization lives for only a short period of time, and this is usually measured in seconds. It is exchanged immediately for an access token so that we can make sure that things are working well. We can start the whole process from our home page.

At this time, our API request to the /token will return an access_token. The property "*expires_in*" should now be set to a variable, and this will represent the number of seconds until the expiration of the access token. This is shown below:

```php
public                                     function
receiveAuthorizationCode(Application $app, Request
$request)
{
    // ...
    $request = $http->post('/token', null, array(
        'client_id'    => 'TopMan',
        'client_secret'                        =>                    '
b3t4f02abc711095f77f2gc04ecbd0d3',
        'grant_type'   => 'authorization_code',
        'code'         => $code,
        'redirect_uri'                    =>                $this-
>generateUrl('coop_authorize_redirect',       array(),
true),
    ));

    // making a request to our token url
    $response = $request->send();
    $responseBody = $response->getBody(true);
    $responseArr   =   json_decode($responseBody,
true);

    $accessToken = $responseArr['access_token'];
    $expiresIn = $responseArr['expires_in'];
}
```

That is it.

How to use the Access Token

We now need to make use of an access token so as to make the API request. One of our endpoints is the "/api/me." This just gives information about the user who has been tied to our access token. We now need to make a "*GET*" request at this end point, and the access token will be set to the "*Authorization*" header. This is shown below:

```php
public                                          function
receiveAuthorizationCode(Application $app, Request
$request)

{
    // ...
    $accessToken = $responseArr['access_token'];
    $expiresIn = $responseArr['expires_in'];

    $request = $http->get('/api/me');
    $request->addHeader('Authorization',          'Bearer
'.$accessToken);

    $response = $request->send();
    echo ($response->getBody(true));die;
}
```

To try this, just go back to your home page and then click on "*Authorize*" link. If you just refresh the home page, it won't work. The reason for this is because the authorization code will have already expired. This is why you have to go back to the home page, find the "Authorize" link, and then click on it. If all is working well, you should see a JSON response having all of the details about the user. This is shown below:

```
{
  id: "2",
  email: "johnjoel@mysite.com",
  firstName: "John",
  lastName: "Joel"
}
```

This will work effectively since the access token that we are using is tied to John's account. After redirection of the user, we will have asked for the profile scope.

Chapter 4- Saving Token

The access token should be stored in case there is a need for us to make the API requests on behalf of the user John.

How to Save the Access Token

Access tokens which last for a period of either 1 or 2 hours are best stored in sessions. Others, such as the one for Facebook, last for a long period of time of up to even 60 days. These are well stored in a database. If we store the token in either way, we will save much of our time, since we will not keep on asking the user to authorize the token. In this case, we are going to store the access token in a database. This is shown in the code given below:

```php
// src/OAuth2Example/Client/Controllers/OAuthContr
oller.php

public function recAuthorizationCode(Application $app, Request $request)

{
    // ...
    $meData = json_decode($response->getBody(), true);

    $user = $this->getLoggedInUser();
    $user->coopAccessToken = $accessToken;
    $user->coopUserId = $meData['id'];
    $this->saveUser($user);

    // ...
}
```

The above code is specific to my own app, but what I have done is that the column *"coopAccessToken"* in the user table has been updated for the user who is currently authenticated. The property *"coopUserId"* has also been saved, since we will need it. This is because most of our API calls have the ID of the user in the URI.

How to Record the Expiration Time

The time at which our token is expected to expire can also be stored. An object which will store this should be created and then used for that purpose. One can try to check on it before they can make the API request. In case the token is found to have expired, then the process of authorization of the user will have to be undergone once again. If not, they can just continue without to go through the authorization process. This is shown in the code given below:

```
public function recAuthorizationCode(Application $app, Request $request)
{
    // ...
    $expiresIn = $responseArr['expires_in'];
    $expiresAt = new \DateTime('+'.$expiresIn.' seconds');
    // ...
    $user = $this->getLoggedInUser();
    $user->coopAccessToken = $accessToken;
    $user->coopUserId = $meData['id'];
    $user->coopAccessExpiresAt = $expiresAt;
    $this->saveUser($user);

    // ...
}
```

Note that the code that I get will be special to my app, so you should get a different one for your case. After executing the above, it will run and then the *"die"* statement will be hit. Once you go to the homepage of the app, you will notice that the COOP user id will have been saved.

Authorization Failure

Sometimes, the user may fail to authorize our app. If this happens, the user will be redirected to the *"redirect_uri"* by the OAuth server. In case we begin from the home page but we are denied access into the COOP, this can be seen. At this time, you will note that the page will explode, since our request to the *"/token"* returns no token.

We should not always assume that the user has authorized our application. In case the authorization fails, the server will always give us information regarding what happened. The provided parameters for error description will be the *"error"* and *"error_description."* You will be the given the type of error which has occurred together with a brief description on what it is.

Consider the code given below, which shows how this is done:

```
public function recAuthorizationCode(Application $app, Request $request)

{
  // similar to $_GET['code']
  $code = $request->get('code');

  if (!$code) {
    $error = $request->get('error');
    $errorDescription          =          $request->get('error_description');

    return $this->render('failed_authorization.twig', array(
      'response' => array(
```

```
        'error' => $error,
        'error_description' => $errorDescription
    )
 ));
}

// ...
}
```

Executing the above will give you a message. Anything can be done in the application, but you should make sure that you are ready to take care of a situation in which the user declines to authorize our app.

Failure toetch the Access Token

During the process of requesting for the /token, things may go wrong. The response that you get might not have the field for the "*access token.*" If conditions are good, then this should not be the case. Consider the example given below:

```
public function recAuthorizationCode(Application $app, Request $request)

{
  // ...
  $request = $http->post('/token', null, array(
    // ...
  ));

  $response = $request->send();
  $responseBody = $response->getBody(true);
  $responseArr = json_decode($responseBody, true);

  // in case we have no access_token, there will be a problem!!!
  if (!isset($responseArr['access_token'])) {
    return                                    $this->render('failed_token_request.twig', array(
      'response' => $responseArr ? $responseArr : $response
    ));
  }
  // ...
}
```

Try to perform the whole cycle again but this time, make sure that you have approved the app. For the first time, the app will function effectively. However, you will get an error once you have refreshed the page.

Redirection after Success

In our previous examples, we have been using the *"die"* statement for the purpose of handling the redirection of OAuth. In our case, we will need to perform the redirection to another page if it occurs. Now that our work is done, our aim is to help the user continue to the next page. This is shown in the code given below:

```
public function recAuthorizationCode(Application $app, Request $request)

{
  // ...

  // redirecting back to our homepage
    return                              $this->redirect($this->generateUrl('home'));
}
```

In the app we have, the above code will work to redirect us to our home page. That is how the authorization grant type works, and it simply binvolves two steps including:

1. First, use the "/authorize" endpoint so as to redirect the user to the OAuth server. The *"client_id"* of your application and the *"redirect_uri"* should also be used. These should be the ones for which a permission is needed. The look of the parameters and the URL may differ on different OAuth servers, but the overall idea will be the same.

2. After authorization of the app, the OAuth server will then redirect back to the URL on our site and have a code query parameter. This can be used alongside the *"client_id"* and *"client_secret"* for the purpose of making an API request to the endpoint *"/token."* At this point, we have an access token.

This can then be used for the purpose of counting. Remember that we have our *"Authorize"* button on the home page. However, this is not needed, since our user has an access token. The template for displaying this page is located at *"views/dashboard.twig"* and a user variable can be passed in here, and this will form the user object which is currently-authenticated. In case the user has the "coopUserId" in the database, we should hide the *"Authorize"* link. This can be done as shown below:

```
{# views/dash.twig #}
{# ... #}
{% if user.coopUserId %}
{% else %}
    <a class="btn btn-primary btn-lg" href="{{ path('coop_authorize_start') }}">Authorize</a>
{% endif %}
```

For users having "coopUserId," we need to add a link which when clicked by the user will perform the counting. What we are doing is simply creating a link or URL which will take us to a page which we have already created. Here is the code for doing this:

```
{# views/dash.twig #}
{# ... #}
```

```
{% if user.coopUserId %}
    <a    class="btn    btn-primary    btn-lg"    href="{{
path('count') }}">Count Eggs</a>

{% else %}
    <a    class="btn    btn-primary    btn-lg"    href="{{
path('coop_authorize_start') }}">Authorize</a>

{% endif %}
```

After refreshing, the new link should be visible. Once we click on the link, it should give us a todo message. You can try it out. You can then open the page "src/OAuth2Demo/Client/Controllers/Count.ph" which is responsible for the user's counts.

Making the API Request for Counting

Begin by copying the code "/api/me" from the CoopOAuthController, and then make sure that you change the method from "*get*" to "*post.*" This is because our endpoint is in need of a POST rather than a GET. This is shown in the code given below:

```
// src/OAuth2Demo/Client/Controllers/CountEggs.php
// ...
class CountEggs extends BaseController
{
    // ...
    public function countEggs()
    {
        $http = new Client('http://coop.apps.knpuniversity.com', array(

            'request.options' => array(
                'exceptions' => false,
            )
        ));

        $request = $http->post('/api/me');
        $request->addHeader('Authorization', 'Bearer '.$accessToken);

        $response = $request->send();
        $meData = json_decode($response->getBody(), true);

        die('Implement this in CountEggs::countEggs');

        return $this->redirect($this->generateUrl('home'));
```

```
        }
    }
```

We are now in need of hitting the endpoint *"/api/USER_ID/eggs-count"*. At this point, the access token and the COOP user ID for the user who is currently logged in has already been saved into the database. To get the data, use the method *"$this->getLoggedInUser()"* and then update the URL. This is shown in the code given below:

```
public function count ()
{
    $user = $this->getLoggedInUser();

    $http = new Client('http://coop.mysite.com', array(
        'request.options' => array(
            'exceptions' => false,
        )
    ));

    $request              =              $http->post('/api/'.$user->coopUserId.'/ count');
    $request->addHeader('Authorization',        'Bearer '.$user->coopAccessToken);

    // ...
}
```

To be able to check on whether this will be working or not, we have to add a debug code as shown below:

```
public function count ()
{
    // ...
```

```
    $request              =            $http->post('/api/'.$user-
>coopUserId.'/ count');
    $request->addHeader('Authorization',        'Bearer
'.$user->coopAccessToken);

    $response = $request->send();
    echo ($response->getBody(true));die;
    // ...
}
```

After refreshing the page, you should see a very good JSON response. We need to make use of *"TopCluck"* for the purpose of making sure that we count for each of the members. This is why a new count has to be saved to the database. You don't to worry much, as all the hard work has already been done. You just have to call the necessary function and then pass in the user and the count and you will be done. At this point, the *"die"* statement can be done away with, and then the user redirected back to the home page once we are done. This is given below:

```
public function count ()
{
    // ...
    $response = $request->send();
    $countEggsData       =       json_decode($response-
>getBody(), true);
    $eggCount = $countData['data'];
    $this->setTodaysCountForUser($this-
>getLoggedInUser(), $count);

    return                              $this->redirect($this-
>generateUrl('home'));
}
```

Once the refreshing is done, the redirection should be back to the home page.

What can go wrong

The page for counting which I have created is working perfectly. However, we have not implemented any mechanism which can be used for handling anything which might go wrong. We have first hidden its ID, but what will happen if the user lacks "*coopUserId*" or "*coopAccessToken?*" The code should be as follows:

```
public function count ()
{
    $user = $this->getLoggedInUser();
    if    (!$user->coopAccessToken    ||      !$user->coopUserId) {
        throw new \Exception('You have no valid COOP access token but got it! Re-authorize!');

    }
    // ...
}
```

I have thrown an exception message, but there is another way how this can be done. A good example is by redirection of the user to the "*Authorize*" page so as to start the OAuth flow.

We also have to check on the token, whether it has expired or not. Remember that the authorization data was stored in the database, and this makes it possible for us to do the validation. An helper function has been created for this purpose. In case it happens, the user should be redirected to re-authorize, since they had clicked on the "*Authorize*" link. This is shown below:

```
public function count ()
```

```php
{
    $user = $this->getLoggedInUser();
    if (!$user->coopAccessToken || !$user-
>coopUserId) {
        throw new \Exception('You have no valid COOP
access tokenbut you got here! Re-authorize!');

    }

    if ($user->hasCoopAccessTokenExpired()) {
        return                    $this->redirect($this-
>generateUrl('coop_authorize_start'));

    }
    // ...
}
```

Sometimes, the API request itself can fail. The method for
handling this can be implemented as follows:

```php
public function count ()
{
    // ...
    $request          =          $http->post('/api/'.$user-
>coopUserId.'/ count');
    $request->addHeader('Authorization',          'Bearer
'.$user->coopAccessToken);

    $response = $request->send();

    if ($response->isError()) {
        throw          new          \Exception($response-
>getBody(true));
    }
    // ...
}
```

Sometimes, one may need to do something which is very complicated. Our response sometimes may have something which has an error in it. You can play around with this. For OAuth2, this might be caused by the fact that the access token has expired. This is why this is important. In real world circumstances, you are not guaranteed that the token will not expire before its time comes. Sometimes, it is also possible for the user to make a decision to revoke your token.

Chapter 5- User Login with OAuth

Creation of New Users

We should begin from the file *"CoopOAuthController.php."* This is the file in which the handling of the exchange of the authorization token to an access token was handled. At this point, we are assuming that the user has logged into the account, and their account is updated with the details of COOP. This is shown in the code given below:

```
// src/OAuth2Example/Client/Controllers/CoopOAuthController.php
// ...
public function recAuthorizationCode(Application $app, Request $request)
{
  // ...
  $meData = json_decode($response->getBody(), true);

  $user = $this->getLoggedInUser();
  $user->coopAccessToken = $accessToken;
  $user->coopUserId = $meData['id'];
  $this->saveUser($user);
  // ...
}
```

But our aim is to allow our anonymous user to actively go through the process of authorization. Once they have done this, a new user should be created in the database. This is shown in the code given below:

```php
public function recAuthorizationCode(Application
$app, Request $request)

{
  // ...
  $meData = json_decode($response->getBody(),
true);
  if ($this->isUserLoggedIn()) {
    $user = $this->getLoggedInUser();
  } else {
    $user = $this->createUser(
      $meData['email'],
      // this is a blank password since the user has
not created a password

      '',
      $meData['fName'],
      $meData['lName']
    );
  }
  $user->coopAccessToken = $accessToken;
  $user->coopUserId = $meData['id'];
  $user->coopAccessExpiresAt = $expiresAt;
  $this->saveUser($user);
  // ...
}
```

Some of the functions defined are specific to my app. The logic is that if no user is logged in, create a new user record and insert it by use of the data from the endpoint "/api/me."

Choosing a Password

In our case, the user has been given a blank password. It will be a huge security threat if the user can login to the app by just proving a blank password.

A password is a good mechanism for one to control how users log into the system. They ensure that your app is very safe. You can prompt the user to choose a password or provide them with an area in which they should provide a password.

Let us begin by logging in the user into our new account:

```
public function recAuthorizationCode(Application $app, Request $request)
{
  // ...
  if ($this->isUserLoggedIn()) {
    $user = $this->getLoggedInUser();
  } else {
    $user = $this->createUser(
      $meData['email'],
      // The password is blank since the user has not provided the password!

      ",
      $meData['fName'],
      $meData['fName']
    );
    $this->loginUser($user);
  }
  // ...
}
```

A few edge cases will have to be handled, but the user has been created, logged in, and then updated with the COOP details.

The login can be added with the COOP link. We need to demonstrate how this can be done. Just log out from the app, and then navigate to the login page. We need to add a "Login with COOP" link here. The template for rendering the page is located at "*views/user/login.twig.*"

The link having the URL should act as the "*Authorize*" button which is in the home page. For those who are already logged in, we only have to update their account. For those who are not logged in, a new account will have to be created, and then they will be logged in.

The database has to be rest completely. This can be done by deleting the file "*data/topcluck.sqlite*" which is contained in the directory "*client/.*"

The following command can be used for this purpose:

$ rm data/topcluck.sqlite

After trying the above, we will be redirected to COOP, then back to TopCluck, and then you will be logged in. Once you check on the details of the user, you will notice that you are logged in as John, and the appropriate ID will also be shown.

Working with Existing Users

If you were attentive, you must have noticed that after login out, if we go through the process once more, we will be done. This is a weakness with our app. What it does is that it creates a second user John other than the first one. This should be fixed. We will create a new private function in the class. If a user is found having this COOP user ID, the user can just be logged into the account. If this is not the case, then a new one will have to be created. This is shown in the code given below:

```php
public function recAuthorizationCode(Application $app, Request $request)
{
    // ...
    if ($this->isUserLoggedIn()) {
        $user = $this->getLoggedInUser();
    } else {
        $user = $this->findOrCreateUser($meData);

        $this->loginUser($user);
    }

    // ...
}

private function findOrAddUser(array $meData)
{
    if ($user = $this->findUserByCOOPId($meData['id'])) {
        // this is the case of an existing user
        return $user;
    }

    $user = $this->createUser(
```

```php
        $meData['email'],
        // the password is blank since the user has not
created the password.

        '',
        $meData['fName'],
        $meData['lName']
    );

    return $user;
}
```

The above code can be tried, and you will get no error. This is because an existing user will be found and no new one will be created.

Duplicate Emails

Sometimes, we might find a user with no such a COOP ID, but with the same email. The cause of this might be that the user has registered with TopCluck, but he or she has not gone through the authorization process of COOP.

A lookup by use of email can be done as shown below:

```
private function findOrAddUser(array $myData)
{
   if         ($user         =         $this-
>findUserByCOOPId($myData['id'])) {
      // the user for this case is in existence
      return $user;
   }

   if         ($user         =         $this-
>findUserByEmail($myData['email'])) {
      // email used for matching
      // Our thought should be on whether to trust this.
      // can the registration at the COOP be done with
someone else's email?

      return $user;
   }

   $user = $this->createUser(
      $meData['email'],
      // the password is blank since the user has not
created it yet.
      '',
      $meData['fName'],
      $meData['lName']
   );
```

```
    return $user;
}
```

However, you have to be careful when doing this. The question is, is it possible for one to fake an email address of someone else on COOP? If this is the case, then I can use the email so as to register and then login to the TopCluck account of that user by use of the same email address. With something else other the user ID for COOP, you have to think about whether the information that you get is correct or not.

Chapter 6- OAuth with Facebook

Facebook makes use of the OAuth2 due to its API. A PHP library is made available which we can make use of. We should install it via composer since the installation method is easy. We have added to the "composer.json".

```
{
  "require": {
    ...
    "facebook/php-sdk": "~3.2.3"
  }
}
```

Integration of the library into a simple application is easy.

Beginning the Redirection

We should begin by adding a link on the home page which will redirect us to Facebook. This is shown below:

```twig
{# views/board.twig #}
{# ... #}
<div class="panel panel-default">
   <div class="panel-body">
     Share what you have on Facebook
     <a href="{{ path('facebook_authorize_start') }}">Connect with Facebook</a>

   </div>
</div>
```

After clicking on it, the code on the first junction will be hit. Our work is to perform a redirection to the Authorize URL on Facebook.

Copy the code given below for our page:

```php
// src/OAuth2Example/Client/Controllers/FacebookOAuthController.php

// ...
public function redTOAuthorization()
{
  $config = array(
    'appId' => 'YOUR_APP_ID',
    'secret' => 'YOUR_APP_SECRET',
    'allowSignedRequest' => false
```

```
    );

    $facebook = new \Facebook($config);

    die('Todo: Redirecting to Facebook');
}
```

Since we are using the composer, the part for *"require"* is not needed. This will take care of it. The application has to be registered with Facebook so as to get both the client id and secret.

Creation of the Facebook Application

Open the link for *"developers.facebook.com"* so as to create a new application. Give it a name of choice and then choose the category. You will then get both the ID and the secret for the app. This should then be added into the code:

```
public function redTOAuthorization()
{
    $config = array(
        'appId' => '1256038998564XXX',
        'secret'                                    =>
'8bc32a48d2bd1988f0d4b9e80a23fXXX',
        'allowSignedRequest' => false
    );

    $facebook = new \Facebook($config);

    die('Todo: Redirect to Facebook');
}
```

User Redirection

The function *"getLoginUrl()"* can be used on the SDK so as to get the redirection URL. The URL that we get will have three important things: the ID for the client, the redirect URI leading back to our site, and a list of scopes which are needed.

```
public function redTOAuthorization()
{
    // ...
    $redirectUrl = $this->generateUrl(
        'facebook_authorize_redirect',
        array(),
        true
    );

    $url = $facebook->getLoginUrl(array(
        'redirect_uri' => $redirectUrl,
        'scope' => array('publish_actions', 'email')
    ));

    die('Todo: Redirect to Facebook');
}
```

For one to know the scopes which are needed, they have to check with the API that they are using. You can Google about Facebook APIs, and a page describing these will be provided.

It is now time for us to redirect the user to the URL. This can be done as follows:

```
public function redTOAuthorization()
{
```

```php
// ...
$url = $facebook->getLoginUrl(array(
    'redirect_uri' => $redirectUrl,
    'scope' => array('publish_actions', 'email')
));

return $this->redirect($url);
}
```

How to get the Access Token

After completion, one will be redirected to the second page, and this has the original todo message. However, we have the "code" todo parameter. This can be exchanged for an access token.

You should begin by creating a private function which will create the Facebook object. This should then be used in both functions as shown below:

```
public function redTOAuthorization()
{
    $facebook = $this->createFacebook();
    // ... our original function part
}
public function recAuthorizationCode(Application $app, Request $request)

{
    $facebook = $this->createFacebook();

    die('Todo: Handle after redirection of facebook to us);
}
private function createFacebook()
{
    $config = array(
      'appId' => '3456038978756XXX',
      'secret' => '7bc32a48f1cf1977e0d4b3f80a24dXXX',
      'allowSignedRequest' => false
    );

    return new \Facebook($config);
}
```

The OAuth will inform us of the next step, which is to make an API request. This should be made to the endpoint of our token so as to exchange the authorization code for an Access code. This is good and to do it, we can make use of an SDK. This is shown below:

```
public function recAuthorizationCode(Application $app, Request $request)

{
    $facebook = $this->createFacebook();

    $userId = $facebook->getUser();
    var_dump($userId);die;

    die('Todo: will be handled after Facebook has been redirected to us);

}
```

Processing this again will give us a user-id which looks as if it is valid. The method *"getUser"* is very useful, as it does a lot of work. It is responsible for finding the code query parameter, and then performs the process of making the API request for the purpose of automatically obtaining the access token. This is very good. Knowing the steps that OAuth2 follows when working will make it easy for you to identify the cause of a problem in case it happens.

Handling failures

As we did in COOP, there is a need for us to handle failures. In case we miss the authorization code or something else goes wrong, the method *"getUser"* will return a 0. Let us demonstrate how the error template can be rendered:

```
public function recAuthorizationCode(Application $app, Request $request)

{
  // ...
  $userId = $facebook->getUser();

  if (!$userId) {
    return      $this->render('failauthorization.twig', array(
      'response' => $request->query->all()
    ));
  }
  // ...
}
```

In case something in our program goes wrong, Facebook will then redirect back to us with information describing what went wrong. The parameters provided will be the *"error"* and the *"error_description."* These will describe the error which has occurred very well, and you will be in a position to take an action so as to rectify it. A good example is when the error you get is *"access_denied."* This will be an indication that the user has been denied the authorization, which means that the process did not succeed. In this app, the queries are just passed to a template which will display them.

We should begin by going to Facebook, and then removing the app from the account. In OAuth servers, there is the possibility of remembering whether the app had been authorized or not. If it had been authorized, the process will not be repeated again.

You can then click on the link for "*Connect with facebook,*" but the authorization request can be cancelled. Once the process of redirection is done, you see the query parameters "error," "error_description," and "error_reason." However, instead of us seeing the error template, we will see the valid userId token, and it will seem as if it ran successfully.

Our OAuth flow has failed. However, despite this, the Facebook object will look for a valid access token which had been stored in the last session which ran successfully. Although this is a nice feature, it is not expected. You just have to know that the function "*getUser()*" will have many tasks to perform. It is the one responsible for exchanging the authorization code for the access token. It can also find an access token which was stored in the last session which ran successfully.

If you need to see your error page, you can clear out the session cookie so that everything is reset. You can then login again and then connect with Facebook. However, make sure that you deny the request. You will get an error page. If it has no session data on which it can fall, the Facebook object will have no access token, and it won't be able to make an API request for the purpose of getting the user id.

How to save the Facebook User ID

After getting the access token in CoopOAuthController, we went ahead to store the details of the user into a database. These details include the access token, the Id, and the expiration date.

In our case, we are in need of storing the Facebook user id. This can easily be done without having to perform extra work, since the Facebook user id will be provided by the "*getUser()* function. This is shown below:

```
public function recAuthorizationCode(Application $app, Request $request)
{
    $facebook = $this->createFacebook();
    $userId = $facebook->getUser();
    // ...
    $user = $this->getLoggedInUser();
    $user->facebookUserId = $userId;
    $this->saveUser($user);
    return                        $this->redirect($this->generateUrl('home'));
}
```

Once we are finished, we are in need of redirecting to the home page. You can now try the whole cycle, and you can approve the authorization request of your application. At this point, you should be aware that a lot is being done behind the scenes.

What happens is that the Facebook object begins by exchanging an authorization request for an access token, and this is saved for the current session. For this to happen, the function "*getUser()*" has to be called. The next step involves saving the Facebook user id into the database, and then redirecting to the home page. Once you click on the box for "*User Info,*" you will be in a position to view the Facebook User Id.

The access token or the expiration can be stored in either the database or the session, and it all depends on what you want. At this point, everything is easy for you. However, when you use a session, you will have to re-authorize once the session has expired. This is why it is recommended that you store in a database.

Conclusion

To conclude, OAuth 2 is a standard used for the purpose of authorization. With it, client machines are provided with an easy and secure mechanism on how they can access the resources of the server on behalf of the resource owner. It provides the resource owners with a mechanism on how to authorize third-party apps to gain access into the resources. These third-party apps will not be required to share their credentials. What happens is that the client machines are awarded an access token by the authorization server.

However, the resource owner has to approve this. The client app can store the access token in either a database or in a session. If you use a session, you will have to re-authorize the third-party app to access the resources once the session has expired. With the case of a database, this is different.

This standard is mostly used when web browsers are in need of accessing third-party websites. In this case, they use accounts in Google, Twitter, or even Facebook. The process of authorization takes some steps. This book explores these steps in detail. My hope is that it has helped you learn more details of OAuth2.

www.ingramcontent.com/pod-product-compliance
Lightning Source LLC
Chambersburg PA
CBHW070856070326
40690CB00009B/1876